I0154560

Playbook to Choose Where Your Life Goes

LIFE SKILLS FOR KIDS FROM TOUGH BACKGROUNDS

Written by Jessica Fincher

Illustrated by Lexi Fincher

Copyright © 2025 by Jessica Fincher

All rights reserved. No part of this book may be reproduced, stored in a retrieval system or transmitted in any form, by any means, including mechanical, electric, photocopying, recording or otherwise, without the prior written permission of the publisher.

ISBN: 979-8-218-71004-0

I dedicate this book to Ire.

Picture the future you want

Table of Contents

About the Author

By the time I was 14 I'd been on probation, shot, suspended, labeled and lost. I had a dad in prison and a mom who never liked me much. At my house, it was kids raising kids. At school, I learned it was easier to ditch and get into trouble than it was to complete an assignment. And, better for my self esteem to avoid than it was to attempt at understanding.

In 10th grade my life changed, but not by parents, counselors, coaches or friends. Thanks to God's grace, I began guiding myself. I started picturing my future, thinking about the kind of life I'd want to live. I began taking action and joined one school sport activity, which led to another, then another. Around the same time, I signed up for multiple school clubs, including Future College Graduates club. This gave me the opportunity to go on field trips touring university campuses. These experiences changed the way I looked at things. I began believing in myself.

I graduated high school when I was 17, moved out, found a job and enrolled into community college. Years later, I transferred to a university. Bartending my way through college, I graduated with an AA, BA and two Master Degrees. In between degrees I became a Program Administrator working in the mental health field. About 10 years later, transitioned to a Program Supervisor in a non profit, supporting kids and families caught up in the foster care system. And my most recent position was a Tier 2 School Counselor in California. Shortly after becoming a counselor, I resigned to become a full time mom.

Throughout my time working in schools, I observed a lot of kids who have so much potential, but seem to be caught up in the whirlwind of life – struggles stemming from their home life, their friend groups, trauma and a lack of guidance. Most of these kids had no trust for the school staff. I don't blame them. I'd say 95% of the time, school staff unfortunately made things worse. This book is a do-it-yourself style approach. Basically a combination of lessons I'd work with the *tough* kids on. Since I stepped out of actual work, I thought I'd put it all in a book. I hope it's helpful and empowering, lighting the fire to motivate you to choose and take action towards your ideal life.

Thanks for reading.

Acknowledgments

Jason, I am so thankful for all your love and support. Thank you for helping make this book possible. Thanks Billy for connecting me to the Stat Girl gig in 10th grade. That pointed me towards better things. Thank you Pop for always being there. Even when you were gone, you gave me more attention than anyone else. I'll never forget it.

I also want to thank the organizations that provided opportunities to not only grow but see life's big picture. To the Cool Program and Milestones, you allowed me to walk alongside you on your journey. Teaching me that being *normal* is a thin line we walk – never take anything for granted. A heartfelt thanks to the youth and families of Wraparound. You welcomed me into your homes and shared your raw and real struggles. You gave me insight into the shadows of poverty and abuse that are so tucked away – out of sight and out of mind for so many. And to all the so-called bad students who took a chance to connect and engage in sessions, your pure gold.

Thank you

©

Part 1

☆ Life ☆

Life

How does life work? Is who we are dependent on where we come from? Try and think about the people who seem to do well in life. You know, those who always seem to have what they need. Who are never involved in drama and always look organized and prepared. How likely is it their parents are organized too? How about the flip side, those people who are always messing up, typically get into trouble and often seem like they're going the opposite way of everyone else. What are the chances their parents are struggling also?

What do you think? Do most of us grow up and live similar lives as our parents and family members? I'm not talking about copying parents' lives, but similar in ways like attitudes, motivation, goals and how to deal with problems. These types of things are known as traits and when passed down, can become a cycle – a type of life that keeps going from one parent to their kids, then from those kids to their kids, and on and on.

This book will talk about ways to break out of a cycle we don't want to continue. Instead, make our live's anything we want it to be. This book covers some of the basic skills that can help change things. In this section, we'll start by discussing life situations such as: growing up, a little about barriers and start thinking about goal setting.

Chapter 1
Growing up

A lot of successful people grow up in an environment that empowers them. Maybe a supportive family that taught organization skills like study habits and how to plan for the future. Or, have adults around who unconditionally love and often suggest they can do anything they set their mind to. If this is your experience, that is a great thing. But for those of us who come from tough backgrounds, childhood is a struggle and honestly can be super sad. Such as; having little to no resources or support, no grown-up supervision and no time available for guidance or attention by any trusted adult.

Growing up in a tough childhood, the main focus may be more on survival instead of personal growth. This is an automatic set back because personal growth allows us to develop our belief system – like what's the purpose of life and how we see ourselves and think about the future. If this part of development is missed, that's a huge bummer making our journey (life) less clear and organized. But, the good thing is, kids from tough backgrounds are strong and can catch up super fast- packing a lot of power behind them.

In hard childhoods, without even thinking about it, most feel destined to continue the cycle we're born into because it's what we know. That cycle might look like ongoing struggle, abuse, addiction, incarceration and barriers. Assuming that's just how life is– while at the same time, noticing the clear differences between us and those other types of people. Those others I'm referring to, are people who go to college, take family vacations, play board games in their living rooms and have what seems to be an easy and happy life. What's the deal? Are some just lucky and privileged, while others aren't? That's absolutely not the case! Anyone can achieve anything. The only thing that matters is whether you have the skills needed. And ANYONE at ANYTIME can learn these skills. That's what this book is about, reviewing skills that kids from tough backgrounds might not have been taught. But by discussing and practicing these skills now– it can be the playbook to make changes and choose where your life goes.

These skills are tools to add new ways to think, cope, respond, plan and take action. These tools ALONG with the strengths you already have can be a very powerful mix. Trying new skills can help shape how we deal with people, problems and barriers– but also how we look at life and opportunity.

Why is this important? It's important because you have the chance just like anyone else to become anything you want to be. Even consider repeating that to yourself *"There is no limit to what I can become, I can choose the life I want."* The only difference is, kids who grow up in homes with parents or caregivers that give them unconditional love and guidance –

4

probably have that statement ingrained in their thinking since they were little. Throughout these chapters, we're going to discuss techniques to learn and practice some of these skills. By the time this book is done, you'll notice even small choices we make have the potential to change our life.

Chapter 2

Barriers

Ever try to do something good, but it never seems to work out? I bet it's because a barrier happened. A barrier is anything that gets in the way of a destination or goal. For example, say you're trying to focus and bring up your grades. However, during class you don't understand what's being taught. Then, when you go home, you try to do homework, but your mom tells you to do other things. When you go back to it– you can't seem to find a pencil or the charger for your dead Chrome book. Once you find something to actually do the assignment with, you realize you have no idea what it's asking you to do. Let's be honest, usually it's easier to stop trying. But when we stop trying, we prevent growth from happening. That's probably a big reason why cycles of poverty and abuse keep going from parent to child and down through the generations. People try to do better, from an assignment to better parenting and self control, but barriers make things hard. So instead of keep trying and working through barriers – often people give in to the wrong behaviors because it's easier. Even though we know we can do better.

Barriers happen to everybody, but for kids who grow up in hard places, a barrier is as common as breathing. A lot of times when we need direction, we might look around and not see any positive influence or role model to ask. So, instead we go blindly, likely setting ourselves up for failure. Or, when we think we made a good choice on our own or decide to take an opportunity, a problem arises and we give up not knowing there's a way to overcome it. We all need direction, but how do we get it?

Picture this example: Let's say, *success* in life is a 5 mile race and *direction* in life is the water. For those who have no direction it's like refusing to give water to a racer. Yet, all the other racers are getting plenty of hydration. Everyone is just trying to make it to the finish line, but there's a clear advantage given to some– while others have an obvious disadvantage. The point is, life is a race everyone's in, and barriers are guaranteed to get in our way. We need to learn new skills that can make any kid from whatever background ready to compete at any time, anywhere. One way to get direction is becoming empowered to create your own path and opportunity. Giving yourself what YOU need to finish the race strong and even win!

What? Even win the race? So we know barriers suck because nothing seems to go easy. But, if you look at it in a different way – what kind of strengths develop from growing up in tough environments? Strengths like a unique insight for truth, a down to earth and real perspective and a natural ability to hold your ground when things get tough. These skills people can't learn from a book, so you already have a huge advantage of your own.

Chapter 3

Future Self

Let's relax and just imagine for a bit. Consider taking a few minutes to close your eyes and think about your future self. Picture your life with no limitations. Ask yourself if you had three wishes for how your life would turn out, what would it look like? I challenge you to shut your eyes and really put yourself there. Can you see it? If not, take some time to let your mind be free to imagine. Imagine the kind of place you'd want to live, what you would be doing for work and who you'd want to marry. Once you picture it, keep the vision in your head, but also put it onto paper.

Next, simply draw three big circles or squares or triangles or whatever. Then label one 20's, another 30's and label the last shape 50's. These numbers represent ages in your life. Inside whatever shape you made, write or draw where you want to live in each of those time periods– in a city, a casual neighborhood, an apartment or a nice little house with a wrap-around porch? Next, in each shape, put down what would you do for work? What would you do for fun? Then, write who'd you want to be surrounded by. You can put whatever you want in these shapes, but the whole idea is visualizing where you see yourself in each of these time periods. Throughout this book and during your day to day activities – try keeping these goals in your mind. When living your life, even ask yourself every now and then, "are my current choices helping me towards my ideal future?"

We'll work more on goal planning in a later chapter.

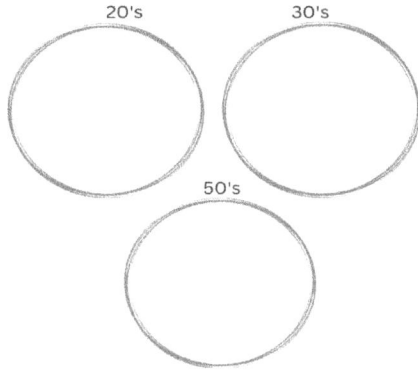

20's

30's

50's

Chapter 4
Choosing a Path

As you read on, each section will focus on a main topic. The chapters in that section will discuss a few skills that support that topic. At the end of each section, we'll look at scenarios to show the potential life impact these skills can make.

Saying that, I'd like to introduce you to two characters, Jessy and Danny. Both come from tough backgrounds. Jessy is a mess. She doesn't know style and has no personal hygiene. She is socially awkward, tries too hard to fit in at school and is being bullied by a lot of kids. She has no role model, barely knows how to read and feels very alone. At home she's like a servant who cooks, cleans and cares for the animals and her younger siblings. Her dad is not around and her mom is always gone "at work".

Danny on the other hand is cool, he walks with a glide and is followed by others. He talks back to his teachers and is quick to fight without asking any questions first. He's failing all classes in school and refuses to meet with the school counselors. He trusts no one and rather be suspended instead of admitting he needs help. He lives with a mom who is rarely home and a dad he's never met. At home, Danny spends all his time on the internet, while the only adult who gives him attention is the junky neighbor next door.

In each section, Jessy or Danny will take two different life pathways– each path will highlight possible outcomes from going that direction. One path is called the *new skills path*, this involves using the skills that are discussed in that section. This route gives the motivation to stop and see things clearly, to decide what kind of future they want. Taking the new skills path is like hiking up a mountain– packing *and* using the skills needed for the journey. This path provides a true view of where you've been, but also a visual of where you want to end up.

The other path is called the *default path*. On this path nothing changes. The default path usually comes most naturally, it's the comfortable path because it's most familiar. Often we're on our default path because that's simply where we started. For example, the choices we make seem to be the same as everyone else in our environment. Our default is like an underground tunnel, we follow it without thinking about what's around the corner, but keep going in that direction because that's what we do.

Let's look at Jessy as our first example. In middle school she was very confused, super anxious and really insecure. She followed any group that would let her tag along. For years she copied what others were doing instead of thinking for herself. In 7th grade she thought she was a chola and in 8th grade she tried to be grunge. She's never completed a homework assignment up to this point and didn't think much about her future. Let's say one day, Jessy took the new skills path and mapped out her ideal future. She started researching how to become a lawyer and decided she better change a lot of things – like doing better in school. She stopped following people and began looking at her life in a new way. She wrote down all her life barriers and started planning ways to overcome them. She regularly asks herself "what can I do now to prepare for next year?" If she did not know an answer, she became a pro at figuring out where to find it. Fast forward 20 years, she grew up to become strong, independent and cool. She became a professional, a leader in her community. She'd often take spur of the moment trips anytime she wanted to. Eventually she got married and had kids. She encouraged and loved her kids so much– Jessy broke the cycle.

On the other hand, Jessy may have followed her default path. Leading her into the cycle she knows best, becoming an unprepared mom and an alcoholic struggling to pay the bills. She depends on her toxic neighbor being willing to watch her kids so she can go out. Instead of helping her kids with homework and making dinners, she tries to find things to do to make her feel whole, while still following others. She never inspired or empowered her kids, leading them to repeat the same cycle when they grow up.

In this example of Jessy, it's pretty obvious which path turned out better for her. But the idea is, by setting goals, making choices and working hard CAN change the cycle we were born into.

It's a fact that anyone from any background can do anything in their life. What if you follow your interests and start to take action? Who knows, it could lead you to creating new inventions or ways of doing things. Or, go to college and become a leader in schools, governments or prisons. You can end up in positions to make things better for so many. You have the power to change your life, your family's life, your community and who knows, why not the world?

Moving forward, please keep these four ideas in mind.

1) No matter where you come from you can be anything you set your mind to.

2) No matter what barriers get in your way, you can overcome them and end up stronger.

3) Visualize the life you want and make that picture your focus point.

4) Take charge of your future by controlling which path you take. And in the process, replace struggle, trauma and hurt with unstoppable hope, goals and determination.

Part 2

☆ **Controlling Feelings** ☆

Controlling Feelings AKA Self Regulation

I know the word self regulation sounds like whatever – a word people throw around often making it lose its meaning. But in this section we're going to discuss self regulation in a real way. How losing control actually happens and ways to get control back.

How do you handle your feelings? Do you let your emotions take over, or do you remain in control over your thoughts and actions? The skill of self control starts by noticing our feelings before they get too big, and then to stay in charge of how we respond and react. This skill is known as self regulation.

In this section, we're going to take a look at four tools that can help people self regulate. The first two skills come in a pair, *breathing* and *positive thoughts*. They are both extremely good to use, but excellent when used together. The other two are called the *Flower of Control* and *Check It*.

Chapter 5

Breathing

We've all heard it before: "take a deep breath." And let's be real, when adults say that, it often makes things worse, not better. Let's put that annoying phrase aside and look at what deep breathing really does. To create a visual, make your hand into a fist with your fingers <u>over</u> your thumb. Let's pretend the fist represents our brain. Say the thumb buried under your fingers is the section of the brain called the amygdala. The amygdala is the oldest part of the brain and what cavemen used to survive. You can put your hand down for now.

This amygdala helps humans survive in life or death situations. For sure, this is a great thing to have. But a lot of kids who grow up in tough environments probably work out this part of their brain often – making it like the boss of the brain. Thankfully, the amygdala can help kids survive when growing up in toxic environments like in homes with abuse, trauma and neglect.

> *If you, or someone you know is being abused, the Childhelp National Child Abuse Hotline can help. Call or text 1-800-422-4453,* **or** *look up your areas child abuse reporting number* **or** *call 911.*

Many times problems happen when the amygdala takes over in non life or death situations. So instead of responding in a chill way, the response is at 100 when the situation calls for only a 10. Basically, this amygdala response is the *street* response, leading to outcomes that usually don't line up with success.

Why does this happen? Well, let's make the fist again with your thumb underneath. The four fingers are the parts of the brain that controls reason, logic, problem solving and understanding. When the *finger-part* of our brain is incharge (closed fist), that's a good thing. That's when you're able to consider options and make choices, allowing thinking to happen. However, when we get pissed off, hurt or shamed, those fingers flip open, leaving our amygdala in control– in a pure survival mood. This is when extreme behavior and responses happen. The survival instinct is great when we're in real danger, but in everyday situations, like at school, work, or with friends we want the logical part of our brain to stay in control.

How do we get logical thinking back in control? By simply breathing. A deep breath puts air back into the brain. Oxygen flowing through the brain allows the fingers to close, covering the thumb again. This puts logic and problem solving back in control instead of a warrior caveman brain to call all the shots.

Let's be straight, there are situations we want the amygdala to take over, like in the matter of self defense or protecting others. But not so much in most day to day situations. Consider pocketing that warrior part and only bring it out when you really need it.

Maintaining control of our feelings by self regulating is the key in reaching whatever goals we have in life. Learning to respond as our genuine self, but in ways appropriate for a situation strengthens us to be successful in all types of environments.

The great thing about deep breathing is it doesn't have to be noticeable. A deep breath is simply breathing in through your nose and barely moving your lips to breath out. You can do this without making it dramatic. Do that five times and you'll feel your brain's craziness beginning to settle down. You can do this anytime, anywhere and no one will ever know. Next we're going to talk about the perfect thing to do after taking a deep breath, it's thinking positive.

Positive thinking can be any thought that's positive to you. It could be something as simple as telling yourself:

"I can do this"   "I am important"

"I have control"   "I love myself"

"I'm smart"   "I know what I'm capable of"

"This isn't a big deal"   "I'm better than this"

Or, instead, this thought could be a prayer, such as:

"Thank you God"

"Please help me get through this"

"Please give me the strength and insight I need".

We're going to talk more about a belief system later in chapter 11. But for now, try to figure out what positive thoughts work for you. These types of thoughts allow your brain the opportunity to settle back to a thinking brain, while feeding good energy into the process. This tool helps respond to triggers or situations in a wise minded way – boosting you in the direction of your goals.

This tool can be a lifelong goldmind. Breathing and thinking positively has the power to help us through any situations life throws at us. Being able to calm ourselves to think clearly is a must-have life skill.

Chapter 6

Flower of Control

Control is something that can get mixed up easily. A lot of us have feelings such as sadness, disappointment and anger over situations we think we have no control over, but we might. Or we may get super anxious, annoyed and feel helpless over a thing we try to change, but we literally cannot. Knowing what we actually do and don't have control over can save us a lot of heartache and wasted time.

Here's a helpful tool, but has a goofy name called the *Flower of Control.* This is a visual tool to help keep track of what's under our control. Why is this important? Because trying to control something that we can't is setting ourselves up for failure and frustration.

The first step is to draw a simple flower. In the *center*, write down the things that you, yourself have control over. Do you have control over your family or where you live? No. Control over your friends or the crap that's going on around you? No. How about control over your decisions, feelings and the goals you make? Yes. As you think about it, also use the

21

pedals to write what's out of your control. Usually, the areas we currently have zero control over are what make us most angry. But for each thing we can't control, consider thinking of an option that we can. For example, say I hate school. We know I can't control the fact I need to attend school. But I can control the way I look at it. Consider the outcome if I chose to simply hate what I had no control over. That outcome is almost guaranteed to suck. Yet instead, if I change my outlook on school to make the best of it, that can lead to better outcomes.

Try thinking of the flower visual next time you get angry or dealing with heavy emotions. Stop and think, "what part of this do I actually have control over?" The great thing about the flower visual is that pedals fall off or blow away eventually. Then, we're left with whatever's in the center, and that center is you! In other words, most things come and go, but if you stay focused on what you can control, you become grounded, steady and better able to keep your feelings under control.

After practicing this idea a few times, you might soon look at situations from a higher viewpoint, seeing the larger picture. It's a powerful advantage, because we spend so much time up in our heads, trying to sort out our feelings or situations that we can't control anyway. Instead of investing this time and energy on what we can't change, consider making an investment in the things you can.

For example, a teacher makes a disrespectful comment to you in front of class. You might react in a way that results in being kicked out of the classroom. Or, you can try to look at it from the perspective that you can't control the stupid things that teachers might say, but you can control your response. Say you choose to simply not react. Resulting with you finishing the class period and not giving into the teacher's bullying behavior. Also, you may consider reporting the situation to the principal. Ultimately you would be in control, not them.

Chapter 7

Check It

Ever get so mad that you feel like you're ready to blow. But hours later you forgot what you were even mad about? In this chapter we'll talk about a self regulation skill called *Check It*, a simple way to challenge our thoughts. When emotions take over, they can trick us into believing things are worse than they really are. So before reacting, stop and ask yourself: "Is this really as bad as it seems? Am I seeing the full picture, or just my emotional reaction?"

For instance, I was on my way to pick up my youngest kiddo from preschool. I was running late, within minutes of closing time and I was stuck in traffic. I'm sitting at a stoplight in the middle of crazy backed up cars. My blood felt like it was boiling. I got super stressed out, angry and wanted to jump out of my car and walk instead.

The school was closing and I was already supposed to be there. This is when I first used the Check It tool, I checked the facts. I asked myself, are they going to kick my kid out and put her on the street by herself? Of course not, my child was safe and fine. Things are not that bad. I'll get there when I get there, and I'll be happy when I do. By checking it, I was able to check myself. The facts led me to self regulate instead of letting myself stress out. Then I rolled my windows down, felt the breeze, and turned up my favorite song. I suddenly had peace of mind and became thankful for the time to myself. You can do this too. Just ask yourself, is it really that big of a deal? Is it something you can let go and move on with your life without a negative experience or situation happening?

Chapter 8

Choosing a Path – Part 2: Controlling Feelings

So let's put this into a real life scenario using Danny as the example. Danny is 14, he's in 9th grade and is red flagged at his school because of all of the fights he's gotten into. The most recent fight resulted in the other kid being hospitalized. When Danny returns to school, he's walking around with his friends during lunch. As they're walking, a teacher Danny had last year makes the comment "they actually let you back in, you have no business here" and shakes his head in disappointment.

Let's look at the two different paths that Danny can take, starting with the default path. He responds by saying "F you" to the teacher, the teacher says back "what did you just say? Leading to a larger situation happening, resulting in Danny getting expelled from school. Once expelled, he's supposed to attend the district's alternative school but chooses not to go. Now Danny is moving towards his future as a dropout. He does nothing but sit around all day hanging out with his adult neighbor who sells drugs.

Danny's life became wasted in drug addiction and just before his 19th birthday, he became incarcerated for assault.

Now let's say Danny chose to take the new skills path. Instead, when the teacher made the comment, Danny took a few breaths, told himself "I'm smart, I'm going to keep my mouth shut". Danny chose to only acknowledge the teacher by nodding his head up once and kept walking. Thinking to himself, "that guy is nobody to me." That day after school, he went home and decided to make a plan. He drew a line down the center of a paper. On the left side he wrote down all of his triggers, you know the things that bring big emotions to the surface. On the other side of the line, Danny lists his new three step plan he'll try anytime he gets triggered. Danny's plan: step one, he's going to take at least five breaths. Step two, in his head, says a prayer to make good choices for his life. And step three, he's going to think before choosing how to respond. Within just a few years of working his three step plan, Danny was offered a full paid scholarship to a trade school. He found a nice, pretty girlfriend who has dreams of her own and he saved up enough for a trip to Australia for his 19th birthday.

Before we go, remember this: Emotions don't have to control us– we have the power to take control. The tools in this chapter are small but mighty, and using them can change the course of your life. Everytime you take a breath, choose a positive thought, focus on what you can control, or check the facts – you're working towards the life you choose.

Part 3

☆ **Perspective** ☆

Perspective

In this section, we're going to be diving into perspective. How it's made and how it can grow. Perspective is simply how we look at something. For example, say two people are walking down the street and see a baseball bat. How a person perceives that bat is going to be different depending on their background. One person's perspective when noticing the bat might see it as a weapon, or a trigger that brings back childhood trauma and hurtful memories. Or, on the other hand, one may look at the bat with amazing and happy memories of afternoons spent with family at the park. Perspective is huge, because it helps determine how we act. It's the root behind why we do what we do in our life.

The amazing thing about perspective is that it can evolve and change if you want it to. This section will explore three key areas that help shape how we see the world. These areas are self-awareness, self-talk and belief systems. Each one plays a huge role in steering our perspective. Perspective helps us make decisions. Those decisions lead to experiences, giving the results that determine where our life goes. So, let's get started with self-awareness.

Chapter 9
Self Awareness

Self awareness can be a journey. One place to start this journey is looking at why we act the way we do. For instance, in the last section we talked about our emotions and how to regain control and choose our actions. But in this chapter, we'll talk more about being aware of our experiences and values. This takes self awareness to a deeper level because it's not so much the feelings, but the why behind the feeling.

There's a term called ACE's. ACE's stands for Adverse Childhood Experiences, it's a list of 10 items, basically a checklist of negative experiences that can happen during childhood. Each item that's checked off is a point. Once all points are added, that's an ACE's score. The higher the score, the more childhood trauma you may have experienced.

Knowing your ACE's score can help you understand how childhood experiences shape emotions and decisions. It's a way to recognize past challenges and take steps towards overcoming those experiences. There have been many studies done regarding patterns found in people with high ACE's scores. We won't dive into the data in this book, but it would be a great thing for you to look up. Key words, *studies about ACE's*, even type in *ACE's* and the checklist will probably show up.

Why talk about ACE's? Because when there's trauma and toxic stress, it's likely a person's emotions and feelings, such as trust and safety are not at peace. Instead, they are always on edge. When a kid is always under stress or fear, it might train their body to always be in that super stressed out state of mind. In other words, their insides never get to relax. So what happens when these kids grow up?

Let's look at the chart of a person who has little to no ACE's score. The line represents their feelings. The numbers on the left show the intensity (0 being super calm and 6 being very explosive). The bottom numbers represent time (in seconds). The bottom corner is the starting point, that's basically "the normal" for a person. The normal for a person is also known as a baseline. In this case, their baseline is a zero. They seem to have no stress- probably have no concerns and not tripping on much of anything. But you'll see in their chart, once a situation happens (as the line moves right) let's say somebody talked crap or threw something at them, their anger response goes up slowly. Giving them time to breathe and think

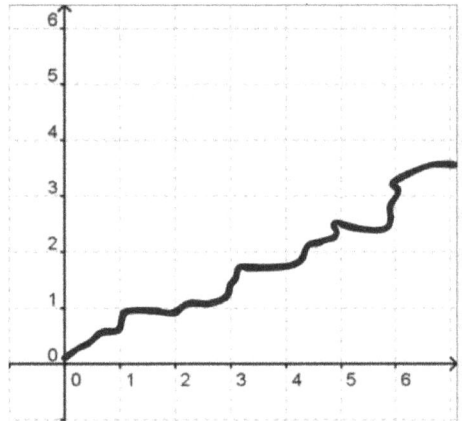

before acting– time to decide the best response or solution for a good outcome.

What about the person with a high ACE's score? It's likely their baseline is always revved up ready to escalate super fast. The next chart represents someone with a high ACEs score. For many with high ACEs scores, their baseline is already high and on edge. This means even small events can trigger big reactions because their body is already in survival mode. For example, those with high ACE's might rarely feel peaceful. Instead a constant state of an uneasy feeling, always looking for potential threats and unable to let their guard down. It's likely, in any situation these kids are confronted with, they are ready to snap. Once a situation happens, they're ready to react without thinking – it doesn't take much to hit the top. This leads to decisions too fast. Not having time to think and breathe, ultimately, preventing the opportunity to make good choices. Understanding this is key to learning how to reset and take control. And the great thing is, no one is stuck– anyone can learn new skills to change this. New skills like becoming self-aware.

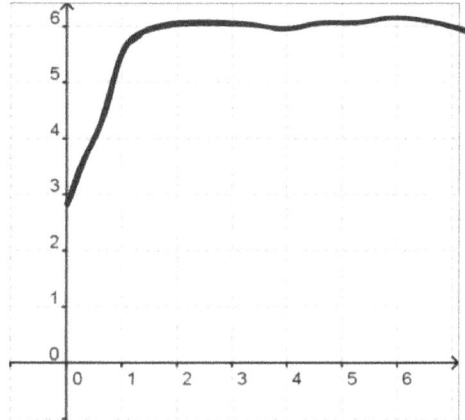

Self awareness can be asking ourselves "what is my baseline?" This is important because we can start teaching ourselves to relax, allowing the chance for deeper thought, learning opportunities and healthy challenges. We don't have to always feel revved up and ready to fight, instead can begin to think about why we feel the way we do. Try asking "is this feeling a normal response for this situation?" If the answer is no, then why?

A quick example of this happened at a training course years ago. Everyone was asked who's their role model and why. Oh my gosh, inside I felt so frustrated. I couldn't think of anyone. While everyone else was talking about their amazing moms or mentors (people who gave advice or guidance), I had no one. I knew my turn was coming up and what was I going to say? After faking my way through that situation. I felt so sad. I realized this one question that was meant to be a positive way to get people talking, created huge feelings in me. This was not a normal response to the situation. The next day, I made my first therapy appointment and began working out my "why".

Other than therapy, a great way to practice self awareness is taking time at the end of each day to think about the situations that took place that day. How did you respond and why? Maybe even think about if you had a re-do, would you have done the same things? If not, what would you have done differently? This is called self reflection and is really powerful because it's rewiring your brain to think in a new way.

Many times, when looking at ourselves and becoming more self aware, it can bring up hidden problems we wanted to avoid. Like situations and events that took place in our childhood or past that may bring up feelings of shame, hurt and trauma. Seeking support such as a therapist to help work through trauma is so helpful. Consider seeking counseling or asking a trusted adult to help find support if you need it.

Need Help?

Any mental health problems or concerns you or someone you know is going through? Like feeling super sad, anxious, extremely angry, or even suicidal? There's help out there. Here's one of many national numbers you can call, the Teen and Young Adult Hotline 1-800-950-6264 or text "Friend" to 62640 or check out https://www.nami.org/support/.

If you, or someone you know is being abused, the Childhelp National Child Abuse Hotline can help. Call or text 1-800-422-4453, or look up your areas child abuse reporting phone number or call 911.

Chapter 10

Self Talk

Don't worry, self-talk isn't walking around talking outloud to ourselves. Self-talk is just *thinking*. I know we discussed this briefly in Chapter 5, mostly in terms of positive thinking. But self-talk, specifically, positive self-talk is being your own coach, mentor, guide and your biggest cheerleader. What we tell ourselves – our brain tries to make it happen for us. There are many studies on this too, how our thoughts can shape our reality. I hope you look it up, key words: *power of thought* or *how thoughts can shape our reality.*

Imagine this: You wake up, feeling bummed, and your first thought is "today is going to suck." But instead, you stop yourself and say, "I can handle whatever today throws at me. I am strong. I am capable." Doing this daily rewires your brain to believe in yourself- and that belief changes everything. By telling yourself things like, you can do anything you set your mind to, you're smart, intelligent, and confident– gives your brain a plan on how to take on the challenges of the day.

Consider challenging yourself to try this every morning for one week. Then ask yourself if you saw any changes happen?

It's super important to be careful that your self-talk is always positive. Most kids from tough backgrounds get hammered with negativity, degrading comments and discouraging feedback. So, it might take a while to get used to thinking positive about ourselves.

Self-talk can help get through a feeling. But it's also about creating a game plan of how we're going to start and end our day. Consider making it a point to end your day with positive self talk too. Even if we screw up that day, we can take care of ourselves by not dwelling on it and instead thinking of ways to improve tomorrow. Then, throughout the day try believing in your capabilities, your strength and your determination – believe in what you want to accomplish. Believing in ourselves leads us to the next chapter, belief system.

Chapter 11

Belief System

Huge populations of the world report life-altering things happen after finding a belief system and living by it. We're not talking about church or religion. Instead, just about having a point of understanding that gives purpose to life. Believing in yourself is so important. But to have a set of beliefs such as the"why" and "what if's" about existence can give us big picture insight – guiding us down our better path. For example, imagine a trip to the store, going around in no rush, looking for the needed items. Might even have a list handy and the money to pay for whatever's in the cart. This is a good feeling, this person has direction with purpose and confidence. On the other hand, say they grab a cart then quickly notice they have no idea what's needed. Ends up wandering around picking up whatever looks good. Although they have good intentions, everything in the cart is crap. Then realizes, no money to pay for the stuff. Although the steps are being made, nothing productive comes out of it.

This is similar to beliefs – having a belief system gives purpose, strengthening the roots of who we are. Naturally standing tall and solid. Yet, while not having personal beliefs leaves us un-rooted. Going wherever the wind blows us – ending up wherever we land.

Try putting this into actual life situations. How would having beliefs help prepare us to make decisions that can change our life? Situations like: drugs or no drugs, sex or wait until way later, work hard or break the law. For sure, situations happen everyday and oftentimes we might make the wrong choice. But, even when we mess up, a belief system helps us stop and turn it around towards good again. It helps us get back up, stay up and remain strong during hard times. It's the fuel to re-start, re-invent and know we can do it. Without something to believe in, it's easy to feel alone and powerless. But believing is like having personal power larger than ourselves, often leading to a better life.

What are your beliefs? I know this is a heavy topic, but an important one. If your considering looking into it, try searching:

How does believing in something change your life?

How does believing in something bigger than you work?

If you're open to finding a belief system that fits you, but not sure where to start, here a few key words to try:

Different types of belief systems.

How to start believing in something?

How to build a relationship with God?

After doing some research, consider watching the sunrise or sunset and just think…powerful things can happen.

Here's a few faith based songs if interested.

Rescue Story – Zach Williams

O Come to the Altar – Elevation Worship

Chain Breaker – Zach Williams

Nobody Loves Me Like You – Chris Tomlin

God Really Loves us – Crowder, Dante Bowe

Fear is a Liar – Zach Williams

Chapter 12

Choosing a Path – Part 3: Perspective

Let's put all this into play by looking at Jessy. She was in 6th grade when she told her mom she wanted to be the President when she grows up. With a grin on her moms face she looked at Jessy and said with a chuckle, "people like us don't become president" and went back to what she was doing. This devastated Jessy.

Years later, let's say Jessy chooses her default path. She immediately gave into the perspective her mom shared with her. She stopped herself anytime she began to think big, and would tell herself she cannot do hard things. She was depressed, always feeling like she wasn't worthy of anything good. Her relationships were short and empty and often settled for anything she could get. She didn't work due to ongoing medical problems and barely ever left her home– she felt there was no purpose in life.

Yet, when going down the new skills path, Jessy took on the power of perspective and thought to herself "I can be anything in my life, I know I can". At first, Jessy believed what her mom said. Everytime she thought about doing something big, her mom's words echoed in her head: "People like us don't become president." But one day, she made a choice. No more. She started telling herself, "I am just as good as anyone else."

And with every time she repeated it, she believed it a little more – until one day, she knew it was true. She began building a relationship with God, going by herself to youth groups and to church camps. She radiated positive and strong energy. She created a confident and thankful life, taking on so many adventures and opportunities over the years. Eventually passing on her powerful perspective to her own children.

To conclude this chapter, when kids from tough backgrounds try to break the cycle, it seems like the moment negative feedback comes or a failure of some kind, it's easy to backslide and give up. This might be a lifelong challenge. A challenge to keep your core strong – away from self doubt and self destructive behavior.

Breaking the cycle isn't easy- but it's possible. When life throws negativity at you, when setbacks make you want to quit, choose perspective. Choose to believe in yourself. Focus on self-awareness, positive self-talk, and a strong belief system.

YOUR future is in YOUR hands- what will you do with it?

Part 4

☆ **Growth Mindset** ☆

Growth Mindset

Welcome to the growth mindset section. There's an 80's band called The Fixx who plays a song titled: One Thing Leads to Another. What do you think about that idea? Can making one choice lead towards a series of events that otherwise wouldn't have happened? If this was the case, where's the first step towards good things happening? And what happens when that first step is hard, scary or you mess it up– Do you keep going? Growth mindset says you do. This section will explore what a growth mindset is all about and discuss a few tools that can help introduce growth mindset in your life. These tools involve being open to vulnerability, taking chances, seeking feedback and considering the cost.

If you stop and look around you I'm guessing you'll see many man-made things. Each and every object we use and enjoy probably took someone a lot of trial and error to create. I'd bet no inventions were perfect the first time. Inventors probably failed tens to hundreds of times before getting it right. It seems like they all had a growth mindset before it was even a thing. A growth mindset is taking a mistake or setback and turning it into a chance to learn and improve.

Think about it– as babies we don't just get up and start walking. It's a process that starts off very basic, standing up at first and with time and practice, walking starts to happen.

Wouldn't it be unnatural if a baby tried to walk for the first time and failed, then never tried again? That would be weird, instead babies are encouraged and expected to get right up and try again. This is a growth mindset at its basic form. How about learning to write? As kids we don't pick a crayon and suddenly be able to write our name. It takes a lot of practice. So, why would anything else in life be any different? The strange thing is, as we get older it feels like we're supposed to get things right the first time and if we don't we feel dumb. Or, when things get difficult or we mess up, it's easier to quit. A growth mindset gets rid of the giving up option and replaces it with being open to correction and even failing because it's an opportunity to grow.

Growth mindset is feeling comfortable with making mistakes and trying new things. Practicing growth mindset is a game changer because once we try and miss, then try again, our brain realigns to problem solve and overcome— creating brain connections that strengthens critical thinking, creativity and develops a problem solving outlook. Not to mention the magic of opportunities that we'll discuss later in this section.

On the other hand, a fixed or closed mindset stops trying when things get hard. It's like thinking inside of a box or a bubble known as the comfort zone. In the comfort zone, we avoid challenges, failure and what people think about us. This mindset does not support growth, instead, creates self made limitations.

What if you were asked to try out for the debate team? Would you do it? With a growth mindset you'd say, "sure, I'll try it". A closed mindset on the other hand would be a simple "no." What answer comes more naturally? Probably saying "no", because then, you know what to expect. When you say "no", nothing happens, your day stays the exact same as before. This often makes people feel secure. But, by saying "sure" it opens the door for an unknown outcome. Who knows, you might find out you're a natural, with big ideas and opinions. Suddenly, learning how to use your voice effectively with the platform to be heard. Or you can look funny, hate it and never do it again, but at least you tried.

Growth mindset suggests regardless of how it goes, just the experience alone offers an opportunity to grow stronger, wiser and better equipped for the next thing that comes up. This all sounds great, but let's be honest, jumping into the unknown takes a lot of courage and guts– and it takes "guts" to be vulnerable.

Chapter 13

Vulnerability & Taking Chances

Allowing ourselves to feel vulnerable involves choosing to take action in situations where we don't know the outcome. Basically, you're putting yourself in a position that might not turn out successful, but you still are willing to try it. In some dynamics and scenarios being vulnerable is not safe. Such as in negative situations we cannot control and/or have no power over. But, in this chapter we'll be talking about vulnerability in terms of a growth mindset. Involving positive and safe opportunities and environments.

One way to see vulnerability is kind of like putting yourself on top of a block wall. Elevated from everyone else. Where everyone can clearly see you– your actions, response and the results. It would even be easy for someone to try to knock you down. Being vulnerable is like being that person up there, you're taking a chance, becoming the target for outcomes, good or bad. But why is this a good thing? Being vulnerable is important for a growth mindset because you're not afraid of the "what if's" or the potential to fail. Instead, you get

49

right back up and try again. By doing this, fear no longer has control. This feeds the mind to grow connections that want wellness and opportunity– becoming empowered to naturally take chances.

By taking a chance and making that first step towards something positive and new, you're opening up one "thing" that can "lead to another". Let's put this into an example, you're bummed, laying around all day on a Saturday and having no motivation. Then someone calls you to meet up at a pizza place down the road. Even though you're not in the mood, you challenge yourself to get cleaned up and go. When you open the door to go in, you bump into someone who's walking out. That someone, you find yourself talking to for a minute and before you know it, becomes an hour. You're in love. Maybe this relationship lasts for weeks or forever, but the idea is this huge part of your life would not have happened if you did not take the first step and go in the first place. When you take a chance, you're evolving by putting yourself in situations that attract opportunity.

Can you think of an example of this happening in your own life? How did it turn out? Or is there a time you regret not taking action? Consider challenging yourself to take a chance that puts you in a vulnerable situation– like raising your hand and participating in class, trying out for sports, summit that application you've been thinking about or even reaching out for support like calling a hotline or a church Pastor to find caring support.

Most of us know, when taking a chance, it's unlikely to go smoothly or the way we hoped to at first, so prepare to be kind to yourself. Going back to previous sections, keep your goals close and perspective strong– having positive self talk ready and a belief system close to heart. After all, choosing your mindset is an adjustment that goes against protecting ourselves from vulnerability and instead, becoming a warrior to the idea of taking chances.

Chapter 14

Seeking Feedback

Another tool that promotes a growth mindset involves seeking feedback. Feedback is welcoming and appreciating both positive and negative thoughts from other people. Thoughts about us, like what we're doing or planning. This sounds kind of crazy right? Why should we care about anybody's opinion? We shouldn't, instead we should focus on our own perspective, goals and mindset right? Absolutely! But the thing about feedback is it opens the window to let in a fresh breeze. In other words, feedback provides a different perspective. This can help keep our thoughts fresh with new insight we wouldn't have otherwise. Not to take anyone's opinions to heart, but if the feedback is coming from someone you respect and trust – their opinion might be super helpful.

Honestly, one problem with feedback is it usually involves others sharing the flaws of our ideas, behavior and/or actions. However, if we're open to hearing them out and willing to take a second look at our choices, goals or whatever it may be – it has the potential to move us forward as a wiser person. Say someone gave us a warning about how we're acting. It might make us rethink it and prevent us from going down a stupid road. Instead of dealing with the outcome of a mistake, we can now avoid it because we were open to feedback.

For example, a kid goes to their counselor saying "I want to go to a college on the beach." Their counselor asks "do you know what college?" The kid says "no, just any college that's on the beach". The counselor asks "what's your major going to be?" and the kid says "I don't know." The counselor might ask "can I give you my feedback?" If the kids say yes, the counselor may share that going into debt by attending an out of town college just because it's on the beach may not be the best plan. Instead, consider the local community college first. This could prevent debt, with the option to transfer once a major is decided. Then figure out what colleges are best for that field." In this case, the counselor's feedback might bounce off the kid. But, if the kid has a growth mindset to feedback, this could help change their course of action. Saving a lot of time and money while creating better outcomes.

How about you? Think of a positive, trusted adult or person you'd consider asking "do you have any feedback for me?" See what they say. If you ask this question randomly, they might not know what you mean– so be prepared to break it down for them. Good luck!

Chapter 15

Considering the Costs

Okay, so we know a growth mindset can change our future, but it also comes with risks. We take a chance when trying something new, especially something that's outside of our normal circle of influence. Circle of influence is similar to the Flower of Control in Chapter 6. It's the people and things around us like friends, family and our environment. Just by being human, we tend to do similar activities and behavior as those around us. This is where the *cycle* mentioned in earlier chapters comes in. By making similar choices to those around us, we continue the path our parents and environments are on. However, by using a growth mindset, it will disrupt the cycle leading to reactions from those around us. These are the costs we're talking about: what can be lost and what can be gained when using a growth mindset?

For example, say you're a part of a group of friends who are known to screw around at school. Never doing class work and always being loud and disruptive. Then one day, you decide to make changes in your life and begin to complete your work and participate during class. It's very likely there will be push back by others. You'd be taking a chance to be judged and messed with by your friends. Your teacher and random students might not take you seriously and you'll probably feel overwhelmed when trying to understand the assignments at first. Longer lasting risks may involve becoming an outcast by your friends, might even become bullied for thinking independently and not like the rest of the group. Family members might even put you down if you attempt to change your priorities towards positive things and even intentionally try to distract you. But with a growth mindset, you can see the larger picture – change is part of the process to choose where our life goes.

By taking risks like these, we win big in the end. Because it gives us the power to take charge of our life. Instead of following, we walk tall and independent. Instead of being a victim or a product of our environment, we become strong and empowered. Being faced with push back from those around us can be hard and super hurtful. But if we are willing to put it in its place and keep focused on what we can control, things often become a domino effect. This goes back to that song title "One Thing Leads to Another."

Chapter 16
Choosing a Path - Part 4: Growth mindset

Let's look at Danny, he runs around with friends who are troublemakers. Everyday he goes to school and is never prepared. He has all F's but somehow keeps moving up to the next grade. He never has an expression on his face and inside he feels very sad. One day during lunch, a new staff person at school came up to him and his friends and asked "hey guys, I'm opening up room 609 during lunch all week, calling it The Nest." Stating, "in there we play games, meet new people and basically socialize in a fun environment. Are any of you guys interested?" Danny as well as his friends laughed and made a joke like "yeah right" before ignoring the staff.

Let's first look at Danny's default path. Say he follows his friends' lead and refuses to engage with the staff and her lunch group. He continues living his life never taking chances – never engaging, interacting or participating in anything new. He graduates high school and has no future plan. He finds it hard to be happy, in and out of inpatient treatment for substance abuse and mental health issues. He has unstable housing, often renting rooms at random houses. In his 30's, still avoiding going outside his comfort zone, finding it impossible to have motivation or structure to do more with his life.

On the other side when Danny took the new skills path, the next day he stopped by room 609 and peeked in during lunch. The staff greeted and invited him in. He took the chance and went in. Soon, he was asked to play a card game with some random students. Danny said "I've never played before, but sure I'll try it." Within 10 minutes Danny couldn't help but smile. The next day Danny walked into that staff's office asking to talk with her, he felt he could trust her. He told her about his recent thoughts of suicide and asked for help. He joined the staff to call home to tell his mom what's going on. Danny's mom wrapped support around him and immediately found him help. After Danny was safe and situated, he was open to feedback. He agreed to meet with the staff weekly for updates, goal setting and conversation. Outside of school, he followed through with taking care of ongoing mental health needs. He began engaging in school and met new friends who introduced him to football. He began playing

football everyday during lunch with random people. The next year, he made the high school football team. He earned solid grades and enjoyed school. After high school, he ended up playing football for the local community college. Danny got hired by the local water company, then within a few years, got promoted and by his mid 20's was making good money and stable. He continued taking care of his mental health throughout his life and built a home and a family he was proud of.

As Danny demonstrated, a growth mindset is not a script to follow or a list to check off. It's a mindset to be open to possibilities that can lead life towards unlimited opportunities. It's so easy to keep doing what we know best and avoid challenges. But instead, when you're confronted with an opportunity or experience that looks interesting and positive, consider telling yourself, "why not" and see where it takes you. We gotta start somewhere… With a growth mindset we can deal with vulnerability and the risk of taking chances– we can welcome all kinds of feedback because we know who we are. And not afraid of the relationships that might be lost, but instead focuses on what can be gained. Remind yourself that you're tough. Live YOUR life on YOUR terms because you have unlimited potential.

Part 5

☆ **Options** ☆

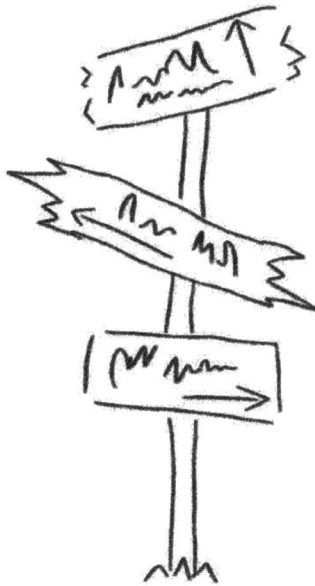

Options

Have you ever sat in a presentation where someone talked about College and Career Readiness and had no idea what the heck any of it meant? I don't know about you, but even the term *college and career readiness* bugs me. How can we talk about readiness when everything seems like a big confusing thing? It reminds me of carrying around an empty backpack. You know, we have it– just like counselors talk about college and career readiness, but both the presentations and the backpack are not actually useful. Both look or sound good, but at the end of the day we're still empty handed. This section creates a safe space to discuss what's-what with all the career and college stuff. Stuff like the different *letters* in college degrees, the different types of colleges, ways to learn a trade and a bit about the Armed Forces.

Why is this chapter a good one to talk about? It might sound boring and not even seem like a skill, but it is. Knowing our options and making choices *on purpose,* is an important skill and a very powerful one. By knowing what options are out there and making choices that fit us best– is exactly what breaks the cycle. This puts the control in our hands, to choose our path. Remember Chapter 3's shapes? The ones we titled 20's, 30's and 50's with goals inside? This section will review the different pathways we can take to make goals into reality. We'll talk more about goal setting in chapter 22.

Chapter 17

Colleges

College talk can be confusing. This chapter will break down what a lot of it means. Like what a *major is,* what the letters representing degrees are all about, and the different types of colleges. Let's get started with a *major* and how that deals with the letters in a degree, like AA or BS.

Picture all the classes you've taken in school. What class was (is) your favorite? Say your favorite class is the subject you'd love to have a career in. That's what a major is, simply the subject you want to focus on. Majors come in all different areas from dance to biology and everything in between. Basically, you can go to college for almost any area of interest because everything falls under a major. And each major falls under one of two categories, arts or science.

For example, we can clump all subjects between two separate groups. One group is the A group. This A stands for Arts, and the other group is the S group, standing for Science. Group A has the majors that are big on ideas and discussion, like music, art, sociology, digital arts, political science and writing. On the other hand, the S group has science type subjects that are proven and factual, like math, biology, engineering and physics. Why is the A and S important?

Because, either A or S will be put onto the end of the next topic, degree's.

Degrees can be looked at as 4 steps or levels, usually with 2 years of full time college between each one. As we talk about each degree just add either that A or S at the end depending on which group your major falls under. For example, the first degree is called an Associates Degree (AA or AS), this degree usually takes about 2 - 3 years to complete. Then a Bachelors Degree (BA or BS) takes another 2-ish years. The Bachelor's degree is known as the 4 year degree. Then the Master's Degree (MA or MS) takes another 2 years and finally a Doctorate Degree. There are many different ways to write out this degree, like PhD. Both a Master's and Doctorate degrees have a lot of different letters depending on the area of study.

Fun thought - some say the higher the degree, the easier college gets, because all classes focus mostly on that major. Basically, if you're interested and knowledgeable in that area, it's probably engaging and more enjoyable to study.

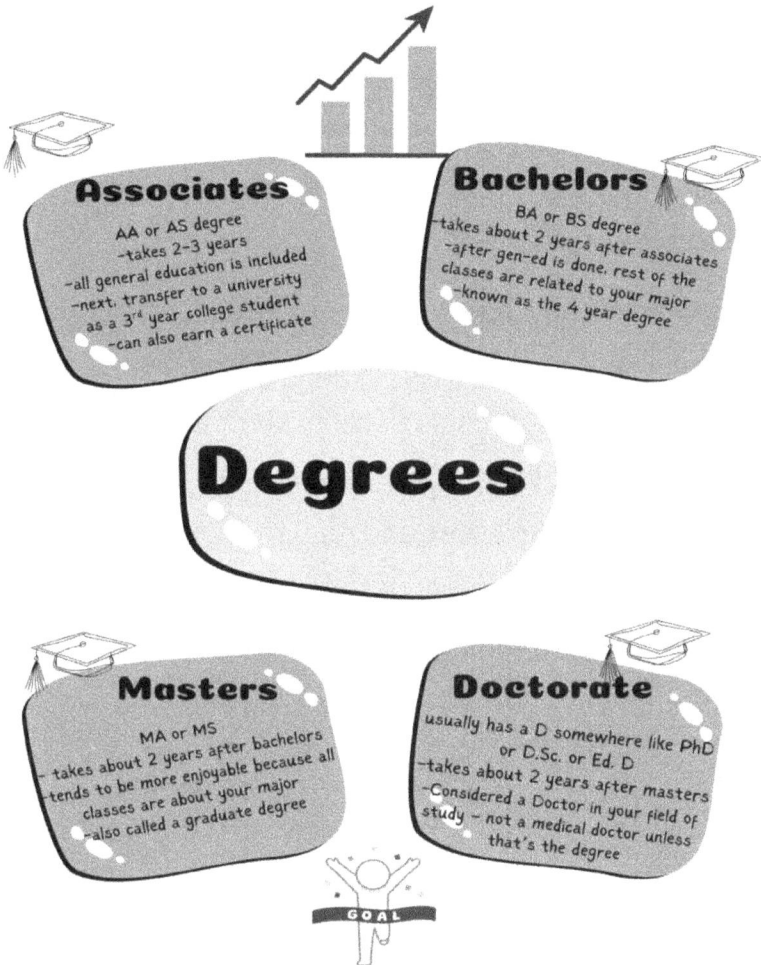

Associates

AA or AS degree
-takes 2-3 years
-all general education is included
-next, transfer to a university
as a 3rd year college student
-can also earn a certificate

Bachelors

BA or BS degree
-takes about 2 years after associates
-after gen-ed is done, rest of the
classes are related to your major
-known as the 4 year degree

Degrees

Masters

MA or MS
-takes about 2 years after bachelors
tends to be more enjoyable because all
classes are about your major
-also called a graduate degree

Doctorate

usually has a D somewhere like PhD
or D.Sc. or Ed. D
-takes about 2 years after masters
-Considered a Doctor in your field of
study – not a medical doctor unless
that's the degree

Now, we'll switch over to the different types of colleges. These are broken into 2 areas. Community college (also known as junior college) and universities. No matter where a student goes to college, the base classes of ALL degrees are the same. These classes are called general education (gen-ed.) These are the basic college classes that everyone has to take the first couple of years. Gen-ed is full of subjects like science, history, math, writing, etc. usually taking about 2 full time years to complete. Different colleges have different definitions of full time. But typically, full time college is 4 or more classes per semester. Semesters break up the school year into two parts, Fall and Spring semesters.

A community college offers all gen-ed classes, but also offers an associates degree and certificate programs. We'll talk about certificates later in this section when talking about trade schools. The great thing about community college is it's a lot cheaper with smaller classes and requires almost nothing to get in. Universities have gen-ed classes too and also offer higher degrees, like bachelors, masters and doctorates.

	University
	• entering requires GPA standards, must complete
Community College	certain classes first and
• enter at any level	might require test scores
• can help get your GED too	• can earn a Bachelors,
• can earn all gen-ed credits	Masters or Doctorate
• get an Assosciates degree	degree
• many certificate programs	• costs more money to attend
• super cheap to attend	• the higher the degree the more focused on the major, no more random classes

Universities cost more to attend and have requirements such as a good GPA, required high school courses and sometimes testing scores like the SAT's. Some people start out at community college then transfer to a university after finishing their gen-ed. By then, they are in their 3rd year of college. This route leads to an easy transition into a university because the admissions process seems smoother.

Universities are either public or private. All states have public universities – you'll see how their names always involve the state and city that university is located. For example, UCR stands for the University of California Riverside, or, CSUSM is the California State University San Marcos. However, private colleges usually don't have their location as part of their name. For example, Howard University or Pepperdine University. Consider looking up the differences between public and private universities.

Next, let's take a minute to call out the obvious, that *college is not for everyone.* There are many non-college paths that lead to great careers. Soon we will talk about trade schools, certificates and apprenticeships. But, before you cross college off your list, I hope you consider this. A lot of people who don't like school, even those who've sucked at school, CAN thrive in college. "What" you might ask? By working hard (turning in all assignments), getting help (using online or school's tutors) and having a growth mindset (willing to keep going) anybody can do college and complete it. The downside is, for some of us who did badly in high school, we may need to start with low level classes in subjects like English and Math before we can reach college level. For example, enrolling into a community college they offer very basic like Math 50, then, we can move up to the next more advanced level, then another level higher, before finally taking a college level math class. This takes longer, but so what! It might take us longer, but the time is going to pass anyway. Is this for everyone? No. But hope you keep the option open. We'll talk about the time and money later in chapter 20.

Chapter 18

Trade School

Let's move on to talk about trades– A trade is learning a specific job, like an electrician, barber or dental assistant. There are so many trades in all aspects of society. Consider running a search on *different types of trade careers.* To get into a trade, there are several different options such as attending a trade school or enrolling into a community college's certificate program.

Trade schools are usually rooms or buildings with half of it being a classroom setting and the other half a lab setting. Usually, the classroom side is just for teaching and book work. While the lab looks like the environment typical to that trade. For instance, if it was air conditioning repair, it would look like a bunch of AC units, or, for office management it would be a few cubicles.

The good thing about trade schools is you can graduate fast. Because a trade school might have class 4-5 days a week with 7 hour days. The downside is, they can cost a lot of money. We will talk about financial aid later, but financial aid often only helps cover a portion of trade school costs. The student is typically responsible for the majority of the cost whether they complete the program or not. For example, once a certain amount of class time passes, students can be locked into the whole price. A trade school can put students in debt from the start. BUT, once a trade school is completed and a job is found, this could be a great investment because money is already being made to pay off any debt.

Another great option is looking at your local community college. Often community college's have many different certificate programs in alot of different trades. These programs are similar to a trade school, however, classes are likely shorter, possibly only a couple hours a few days a week. This makes it take longer to complete. The good thing is, it's significantly cheaper. Your local community college is inexpensive and often free for those who meet the income criteria. This route gives the chance to learn a trade and not fall into debt. If you pull up a community college's website, look for their certificate programs.

Chapter 19

Apprenticeships & The Armed Forces

There's a thing called apprenticeships. It sounds old school and I never hear them talked about, but it is such an amazing option. Being an apprentice is basically getting hired by a professional who pays you to work, while they teach you the trade. You don't go into debt and instead, you make money while learning. Often, apprenticeship jobs are entry level, meaning you do not need any experience in that field to be hired. Consider looking up *how to become an apprentice*. This simple internet search can open the doors to all kinds of possibilities. The downfall to apprenticeships is there might not be many apprenticeship opportunities in your area, especially if you're interested in a specific trade. If this is the case, try daring yourself to call up businesses in your area that deal in the field you're interested in. Ask if they would be open to an apprentice? Even if you can't find an apprentice role, it's likely you might be offered a job...That can be a great start. Even still enroll into community college for that certificate. Talk about setting yourself up for success. Having both the education and hands-on experience can lead to big opportunities, higher pay and more options.

Speaking of pay, another option to gain education and experience is joining the Armed Forces. The United States has

6 branches of the military: Army, Marine Corps, Airforce, Navy, Coast Guard and the Space Force. This is definitely worth looking into because it pays a salary, provides housing, can cover college tuition and gets you out to new places and adventures. It's a way to learn independence, survival, a trade with the opportunity to have college costs paid for. Not to mention, honorably serving our Nation. Recruiter's are almost always available to answer questions with no obligation to join.

Chapter 20

Deciding Factors

Let's talk about two huge barriers that often prevent planning for our future and career– money and the time it takes. There's a thing called the FAFSA, this Free Application for Federal Student Aid. It's used for community college, universities and some trade schools. This is a huge and important thing to complete when considering your options. Financial aid typically offers students *some* money in grants. This money typically helps cover classes and books. Grants are funds the student never needs to pay back. BUT financial aid also offers loans. BE CAREFUL! Loans are dangerous! They seem so easy– basically, you're offered money and when you get the money you do not need to pay anything back until you're done with school.

It's so easy to take, and easy to forget it adds up. Some people finish school, find a job and quickly notice they are in a world of debt…debt makes starting out in life really hard. Why does this happen? Student loans may offer students money not just to pay for classes and books, but money to live on.

Instead, be wise, if you need a loan like many of us do, just cover the basics and send back any money left over. And instead of living off the money given by financial aid, get a job to pay rent, food, ect. By doing this, it makes such a difference.

Time goes fast, but the money we borrow stays with us. Consider avoiding debt as much as possible.

The other barrier is time. A lot of people think college, skill training (trades), military, or apprenticeships take too much time. Doesn't matter if we're talking about 1 year or 8 years, many of us feel there's better things to do with our time. But let's put time into an example and use tonight from 10:00 p.m. until 6:00 a.m. Those hours are going to happen no matter what, right? But, what are you going to do during that time? You might choose to sleep from 10:00 to 6:00 and in the morning you'll wake up and go about your day– done and done. Actually you don't even think about those 8 hours because they're in the past, who cares? But if you choose not to sleep and mess around all night just wasting time, tomorrow is probably going to suck! Now compare that to the next 8 years. Time goes by no matter what...but eventually our life becomes the result of how we spent that time. So when looking at your options, consider not letting the amount of time turn you off too much. It's going to pass anyway, might as well do something with it and live the life you choose.

Chapter 21

Choosing a Path – Part 5: Options

Let's take a minute and talk about Jessy. She was never told about college, had no idea what it was about or how to get there. She scheduled a meeting to talk with her school counselor. She sat down and asked "can you tell me what college is all about?" He told her "you shouldn't worry about it", then he answered his phone. Seeing that the counselor was not interested, she took off.

As Jessy left, say she chose the new skills path: using emotional control, perspective, growth mindset and now wanting options– She walked over to the Principal's office and said, "I want to learn about college, the counselor won't help me, can you?" The Principal walked Jessy across campus and introduced her to the teacher who ran the college club. That day Jessy became a member. Fast forward 5 years, Jessy is

sitting in one of her university classes when she looks around the room. Everyone just nodded along. No one challenged the speaker. No one asked questions. Jessy thought to herself, "some of the dumbest people I've ever seen are in universities." And that's when it hit her. College isn't scary. What's scary is that people who don't think for themselves might be in leadership and professional positions someday. Maybe I can teach them something."

Ten more years pass and Jessy is a boss of a great organization. She trains professionals to build a mindset that actually connects with people. Jessy works full time, but is still available to volunteer in her kids' classrooms, helps coach soccer teams and never misses an award given to her kids. Jessy is now in a leadership position, has a flexible schedule and controls her own time. She has uncovered the lie that college is only for some and not others. Seeing how anyone can become book smart, but not anyone can be genuine and strong.

But what if Jessy hadn't spoken up that day? Probably would have taken her down the default path instead. Say she left the counselor's office and returned to her day as if no harm was done. Honestly, even feeling relieved because the idea of college seemed intimidating anyway. Jessy never considered her options, just fell into whatever job was available. She never had vacation. No sick pay. No requested days off. She worked weekends, holidays, and nights. Her

schedule changed every week. Her kids needed her– but she couldn't be there. She was always working. Always tired. Just trying to keep up. Jessy worked hard and earned an honest living. But the lack of choosing, made time and options not hers to own. Here, both paths were possible. But only one broke the cycle.

In conclusion, nothing is out of your reach. College might appear as a castle off in the distance, but it's not– it's just a bunch of buildings that anyone who's willing to work hard can go to and graduate strong. And, if your goals are not college driven, diving into a trade is a powerful and direct way to begin a lifelong career too. While, for some, the military might be a perfect tool to reach their goals and see the world while doing it. Before leaving, please take with you that time will happen no matter what, use it wisely. As well as money…try to avoid debt as much as possible.

Remember, if you can think it, you can do it!

Part 6

☆ **Structure** ☆

Structure

Picture this, you're sitting in a classroom trying to pay attention and the ceiling is crumbling on your head. It's unlikely anyone would be able to focus right? Because the structure of the building sucks, that's where all the attention goes. But, if you're in a well structured building you don't have to think about the ceiling or the walls, the structure is good and you can focus on what's in front of you.

This is similar to the structure we make in our own lives. If we create a good structure to build our life on, it can help us stay focused on the important things. But, if there's a lack of structure, it can distract and honestly, even destroy success. There are many ways to create structure in our lives. This section will cover just a few which are: goal planning, organization and strengthening problem solving skills.

Chapter 22

Goal Planning

Let's start with goal planning. Goal planning is a secret weapon giving us power over our lives. To do this, it costs nothing, takes less than an hour to complete and thanks to the internet, all the information we need is at our fingertips. Once we lay our plans out on paper, it frees up space in our mind for other thoughts. Goal planning takes three steps. First, figure out what your goals are. Second, figure out the steps it takes to reach that goal. And third, take action.

The hardest part might be coming up with a goal...If you draw a blank, think back to chapter 3's shapes, titled 20's, 30's and 50's. You don't need to use those, but it could be a good place to start. Since then, we talked about alot of topics. So, take some time and think about your goals. As you're thinking, don't let yourself be scared or intimidated by any ideas. We can set any goal we want cause there is nothing out of our reach. It's really important to know that we can make changes at any time and that's okay, actually it's even good. It doesn't matter how many times our goals change or not. Just by having a goal plan and actually working it, creates the structure needed to move forward in the direction we want to go.

Once you decide on a goal, next, find out what steps are needed to reach it. When steps are laid out, this can easily become overwhelming, especially if it requires significant time or effort to achieve. Instead of feeling defeated, consider looking at it in a way you can relate to, like making a meal. For example, all the steps to make breakfast can look like a lot! Such as cooking the eggs, making the sausage, mixing and flipping pancakes and cutting fruit. A meal doesn't just happen, it takes work. By doing one thing at a time, before we know it, we can sit back and enjoy it. Or, we can look at it from another perspective, as an eater. Of course we can't put a whole plate of food in our mouth at once. We need to take one bit at a time. After eating so many bits, our meal is done. Same thing with goals. By breaking goal planning into steps, it becomes a bit size action plan. We know the time will pass anyway right? So, if we keep moving & working effectively – any goal can be reached.

To try it, just write a goal at the top of a paper. Then, find out the different steps required to reach that goal and write them down. Also, consider adding your own steps to match your values. Such as eating well, staying single, saving money, etc. As you accomplish each step, check

or cross it off. For example, if the goal was to get a certificate in automotive repair and buy a house, the planning could look like these two examples.

A great way to keep focused is placing the goal plans in a place where you see them everyday, like on the wall or as a screensaver. Or, consider making a vision board, keyword: vision board images. These are snapshots of our goals and a great visual motivator. As long as the actual goal plan that involves the steps needed is kept somewhere close.

Another way to goal plan is making a step by step to-do list. For example, if the goal was to work as a preschool teacher, the goal plan may look like this.

	I need to:	How:
Step 1	Enroll into community college	Apply on website
Step 2	Fill out FAFSA	studentaid.gov
Step 3	Find part time job	Online search 1 hr. Daily Walk in w/ resume 10 places a day
Step 4	Buy a car	Find used car, pay in full with next year's tax return
Step 5	Start program	Take early childhood dev. Classes. Earn Associate's degree
Step 6	Get experience	Offer to volunteer or intern at preschool or day care

Your goal plan can take any form, as long as it shows actual steps that move you towards reaching the goal.

As months and years go by, simply update goals as needed. For example, as we gain new experiences and as new opportunities come up – our goals might change. This is good. Actually, some say that's great because as we're exposed to more– more ideas and options open up. Updating our goal plan can be as easy as replacing one goal with a new one, or simply adjusting as changes occur. But keep in mind, when goals begin costing money like trade schools or college, it's a good idea to do research and maybe even shadow a day in that job before committing. Because, changing later in the game becomes difficult in debt-creating situations.

Chapter 23

Organization

Most of us naturally want to avoid the idea of becoming organized. Organizing can be as simple as making a routine, to as hard core as creating systems to manage stuff, ideas and time. No matter what level feels comfortable to you, just being somewhat organized can help keep life's must-do-tasks smooth and simple instead of stressed and scattered. In this chapter, we'll talk about two organizational approaches. The first approach is called the *folder stack* and the other is the *steering wheel.*

Let's start with the folder stack method. This is simply getting at least 6 different colored folders and assigning each color a subject, topic or goal. In each of these folders put anything that deals with that "thing" inside. For example, having a folder for each class is helpful because most classes have finals that cover all material from the beginning to end. By keeping all notes and assignments in one place makes studying become a lot easier and more effective. Other things that are good to keep organized are paperwork like pay stubs (work folder), school records (school folder),

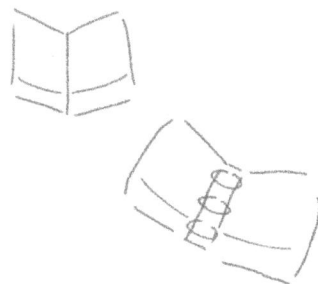

medical info and dates, personal records like a birth certificate (vital documents / medical folder), bank stuff (financial folder), etc. This method can be applied to digital folders on a drive, computer or email too. By using the folder stack method, it puts everything about one thing, inside one spot.

On the outside of each folder consider taping a paper to the front. On this paper, you can create a to- do list, notes or anything you want about that folder. This helps keep track of what's what and what's next while creating good book keeping habits for life.

Let's talk about notes for a minute. Notes can be just one line that includes the date, who you talked to, and a summary of what was accomplished. For example, say you talk to a teacher about how you're unable to open an assignment. Each time you talk about the problem, note the date and the outcome. Because, often we may need to remember these types of conversations at a later time. By taking notes of when and what was said, you can advocate for yourself and get things done. For instance, say that the teacher gave you a zero on that assignment. Now, you can address it with exact details that puts you in a position of facts, instead of being looked at as a powerless student. This type of organization helps overcome obstacles and take charge of what's happening around us.

Next, let's talk about day to day organization. This method is called the steering wheel. All it takes is using one piece of paper each week. Basically turn a paper long ways and draw 4 or 6 lines from the top to bottom. 4 lines if you want weekdays only, or 6 if you want weekends included. Then draw one line across the middle. At the top write the days of the week. Then in each column write "TO DO" and on the bottom half write "NEEDS". Or, can simply use a calendar to write on instead.

Monday	Tuesday	Weds	Thursday	Friday
To do:	To do:	To do:	To do:	To do:
Needs	Needs	Needs	Needs	Needs

Under the TO DO, write the things you have to do. This can be tasks, like homework, making appointments, doing laundry, sport tryouts, cleaning, looking for a job or even getting to school or work on time.

The NEEDS are things that come up when you're working on the TO DO's. Like when doing homework and don't get it. The NEED can be to get a tutor or talk with a teacher. If a TO DO is finding a job, the NEED can be to make a resume (keyword "how to make a resume"). As you complete To Do's or NEED's, just cross them off. This is a quick and easy way to organize what needs to get done and motivates us to keep moving in a positive direction.

So far, all of this sounds good, planning and organizing but it only works if we take action. And, action takes time. Not just time, but protected time. Protected time gives the space needed to seriously focus and enter into a productive head zone. Whether it's homework, research, resume writing, or planning your goals – finding quiet, uninterrupted time can be a challenge. A lot of us have other expectations, interruptions and distractions that need our attention, especially when at home.

So we know a huge part of structure is finding the time to plan and get things done, but how do we find time? Try to think outside the box and get creative. For example, consider a place like a 24 hour restaurant. There you can have your own table to create a work space while getting refills. Often, as long as you are paying for something, it's no problem to stay for hours. And it provides an environment to easily stay awake. Other common options are coffee shops or a local library. All these options have free wifi and the opportunity to nest in the corner and get in the zone.

Factoring in time and location as a part of our daily routine can create protected time. Say you're at school all day and feel you don't have the chance to get any assignments done. Afterschool, consider trying a routine of going into the library for 1 hour before going home. By focusing and treating it like part of your school day, that could be 5 hours of protected time each week. Or, if you're in college, go into the library before, between and after class to knock out your assignments before leaving campus that day. A great idea regarding college is to select classes held on the same two days instead of spreading them out throughout the week. Like every Tuesday and Thursday. Say the first class begins at 9 am and the last class ends at 9 pm. Classes only take an hour or two each, so this gives several hours between classes to camp out in the library and complete assignments. Do this for two days each week, that can become 8-10 hours of protected time to complete school work. THEN, leaving the other five days of the week to work, volunteer and have fun. Organization and time management, along with a little discipline can make a world of difference in reaching any goal.

Lastly, the KEY in protecting time is putting our phone face down and on silent – we all know phones are a huge distractor of time. By doing the silent, face down for at least an hour at a time, we don't miss anything. Still able to see all missed calls or notifications, just not during our precious protected time.

Chapter 24

Problem Solving

We all know problems and crappy events will happen in life. But the crazy thing is, often when we try to do the right thing, that's when problems pop up the most. We talked about this a bit in the growth mindset section. How it's easier to give in and give up when things get hard. Our brain is wired to repeat whatever pattern we are used to, so let's talk about a new pattern. This chapter will cover two ways of practicing problem solving that can become a new *habit* of finding solutions that support our goals.

For example, say the problem is having no food in the house. One solution may be going to the store and stealing some things. Or the other could be running an online search on how to get food in (whatever city) for free. Both of these are solutions, but obviously one has the potential to lead to a criminal record. While the other may lead to an open door of opportunity and resources that can help struggling families.

Problem solving is a skill and to get good at it, we need to practice. Why is this so important? Because problem solving is choosing! Choosing the type of life, environment and circumstances we are in. We can't choose how we start off, but we choose how we respond– either stay in the cycle we know, or rise above and overcome.

Here's one approach to practice, it's called the *why and what if* method

First, *say what the problem is* "I _____," *then why* "**because** _____." *Think of a possible solution* "**What if I try** _____ **instead?**" *Consider the possible outcomes to that solution* "**Things might** _____".

Let's say the problem is getting all F's– I never get good grades, **because** I don't understand how to do the work. **What if I try** to turn in every assignment no matter if I guessed the answers or not **instead? Things might** change from F's to D's or C's.

Taking it a step further, say we added, what if I try *getting a tutor twice a week*? Things might change because I'd be understanding how to do the work. Could earn A's and B's instead.

Another approach involves a 3 step problem solving method: #1 ask yourself what is the actual problem? This might sound dumb, but seriously, knowing the exact problem and being aware it exists is needed inorder to solve it. #2 How did it become a problem? This is good because it tells you the root cause of the problem. Usually if you go to the root, the real problem can be dealt with. #3 What can make it stop or go away? Here is an example.

3 step problem solving

What is the problem?	=	*My parents are divorcing and I need to move out on my own.*
How did it become a problem?	=	*I don't have any money, no idea where to go. My parents have their own problems.*
What can make it go away?	=	*Find out the exact time frame. Find a job tomorrow, find a room for rent, ask parents what they can do like help w/ 1st month rent. Plan.*

Consider trying these methods a few times. At first it will probably be awkward, but soon, you may notice problem solving becomes a quick and easy mental checklist. These scripts help give our brain a chance to open the door to a natural gift – problem solving our way through life.

Chapter 25

Choosing A Path – Part 6: Structure

Let's put the power of structure into play. At age 11 Danny became a foster kid. He was removed from his mom and bounced from one foster home to another. Each move usually meant switching schools, becoming almost impossible to do well. He felt powerless with no control over anything.

Around Danny's 14th birthday he tried the new skills path and began planning out his life goals. He taped the ends of two papers together so he could fold them into a binder-sized piece of paper and open it like a book. He wrote down his goals and listed what he needs to do to reach them. No matter where he lived, or if his mom completed the requirements to get him back or not, he took power over his life. He made a plan for himself that no one could mess with. He ended up graduating high school and became a roofer's apprentice. Danny started his own business at age 26 and became a leader in his community by mentoring and training any foster kid willing to learn and work hard. Motivating them to choose where their life goes. Within 10

years, some of those foster kids who Danny mentored became mentors themselves coaching others. But now, they're spread out, mentoring throughout the nation. Because of Danny's choices, many lives were impacted for the good.

How about the default path, if Danny simply chooses nothing– no writing down ideas, planning or problem solving… He continues being moved around, not having any control over what's going on in his life. He turns 18 with nowhere to go, no money and no idea where his mom ended up. Danny joined a housing program for aged out foster kids. He found a part time job and developed a daily routine, but lacks a clear plan. By his 21st birthday, he had to leave the housing program. With no alternatives, Danny moves in with his girlfriend and her family. Soon after, his girlfriend became pregnant. Immediately, leading to getting kicked out by her parents. Danny becomes homeless, does drugs to stay up at night and commits crime to get through each day. Unfortunately, Danny became just another statistic.

I agree the word *structure* might be a huge turn off, but it's a pretty big deal. Structure can be the very thing that helps support dreams, goals and ambitions. When looking ahead into your future, think about keeping these three points in mind.

1) Make goals and break them into small steps. Focus on one piece at a time instead of the whole thing at once. 2) Create organization, this can be any kind of method that works for you. Organization also helps create positive habits that are helpful long term. And lastly, 3) Problem solving is a skill that improves over time. Good solutions create good outcomes.

Conclusion

I hope this book helped you see how important you are. We are all unique and made on purpose. No one can tell us who we are, or who we will become. You have the power to choose where your life goes.

"The stone that the builders rejected

has become the chief cornerstone."

Psalms 118:22

www.ingramcontent.com/pod-product-compliance
Lightning Source LLC
LaVergne TN
LVHW090417090426
835511LV00043B/690